Alpacas grazing in a high mountain pasture of the Andes

Wonders of Llamas

ROGER PERRY

ILLUSTRATED WITH PHOTOGRAPHS AND A MAP

DODD, MEAD & COMPANY · NEW YORK

PICTURE CREDITS

Jen and Des Bartlett, 18, 22, 39; British Museum, 52 (bottom), 66 (bottom); Cambridge University Museum of Archaeology and Ethnology, 52 (top), 65, 66 (top); Douglas Fisher, 14; Derrick Furlong, 92; Mansell Collection, 16, 62; Brian Maynard/Artricia Photographs, 89; Marion Morrison, 49, 83, 94–95; Roger Perry, 2, 8, 9, 11, 24, 27, 28, 32–33 (top), 36, 42–43, 45, 63, 68, 71, 72, 73, 79, 82, 85, 86; Poma de Ayala, *Nueva Corónica*, 15, 57; Courtesy of Juan Preloran, 37; Royal Geographical Society, 78; Jean-Christian Spahni, 56, 58, 81; Ian Strange, 76; W. L. Franklin/A. Stokes, World Wildlife Fund, 44, 93. The photograph on page 35 is from *At Home with the Patagonians* by G. Musters, Courtesy of John Murray (Publishers), Ltd. The photograph on page 33 (bottom) is from *Reports of the Princeton University Expeditions to Patagonia, 1896-1899* by J. B. Hatcher, Princeton University Press (1903).

The author gratefully acknowledges photographic assistance given at the Kilverstone Wildlife Park, Thetford, England.

The map on page 6 is by Dyno Lowenstein.

Printed in the United States of America

1   2   3   4   5   6   7   8   9   10

Library of Congress Cataloging in Publication Data

Perry, Roger, fl. 1972-
    Wonders of llamas.

    Includes index.
    SUMMARY: Introduces the physical characteristics,
habits, and natural environment of the llama, alpaca,
guanaco, and vicuña.
    1. Lama (Genus)—Juvenile literature. [1. Llamas.
2. Camelidae]   I. Title.
QL737.U54P47   599'.736   77–6492
ISBN 0–396–07460–X

Contents

VENEZUELA

GUYANA
FR. GUIANA
SURINAM

COLOMBIA

•Pasto

ECUADOR •Quito
Mt Cotopaxi

B R A Z I L

A
N
D
E
S

PERU

Lima• •Jauja •Machu Picchu
•Cuzco
Paracas• Ulla Ulla• •Macusani
Lucanas• • I *Lake Titicaca*
Arequipa• •Tiahuanaco BOLIVIA
Altiplano •Sabaya
Arica• •Parinacota
•Uyuni
•Charaña

•Humahuaca

C
H
I
L
E

Atacama Desert

M
O
U
N
T
A
I
N
S

PACIFIC
OCEAN

Copiapó•

ARGENTINA

•San Juan
•Mendoza
Buenos Aires•

Pampas

ATLANTIC
OCEAN

Negro River

Valdés
Peninsula

Patagonia

•San Julián

FALKLAND IS.

N
W E
S

0   500   1,000
Scale of Miles

Isla Grande
Strait of Magellan Tierra del Fuego
Beagle Channel Navarino

1. World of the Llamas

The Andes stretch for 4,500 miles as the high mountainous backbone of South America. For two-thirds of this distance, from Peru to the far windswept land of Patagonia, they are the home of a group of animals known as the llamas or lamoids. Since early times, these woolly camel-like animals have been very important to man. They provided food and clothing for countless wandering people, and once man had settled in the central highlands of the Andes they became his close companions. In no small way llamas assisted in the rise of the great civilization of the Incas, whose mountain kingdom stretched from present-day Ecuador, south to Argentina and Chile. Today, many native highland Indians still depend for their livelihood on these graceful yet temperamental creatures.

Lamoids, or llamas (as they are more generally known as a group), consist of the vicuña (*Lama vicugna*), guanaco (*Lama guanicoë*), alpaca (*Lama guanicoë pacos*), and the domestic llama (*Lama guanicoë glama*). Guanacos and vicuñas live in the wild, while alpacas—as well as llamas—exist only as domesticated animals.

In appearance the lamoids are a curious mixture. Their close links with the camels are unmistakable, and they belong to the same family. The general shape of the head and body and the long neck and legs remind one of a scaled-down version of

7

The guanaco was described in Magellan's time as a beast with "a large head, ears like a mule, the body of a camel, and tail of a horse."

Stiff neck, divided upper lip, and long eyelashes give the llama an expression that one feels should not be altogether trusted. Protruding lower teeth help in cropping tough grasses which are its main food.

the camel. But the lamoids are only about a third the size of their great humped relatives of the Old World. Besides lacking a hump or humps, they differ from camels in other conspicuous ways. They do not have extensive calloused areas on the knees and underside of the body which camels develop through lying on the hard stony ground of the desert. The tail is shorter and fluffier, the ears are longer, and the coat is much more woolly. Because of their wonderfully long fleeces, early European visitors referred to alpacas as the "sheep of the Andes."

Another notable feature of the lamoids is their expression. They seem to look down at you in a haughty way, with head high and a half-veiled look through long eyelashes. Hiram

9

Bingham, the American archaeologist who discovered in the Peruvian Andes the lost Inca city of Machu Picchu, wrote that the llama usually manages to look as though its presence near you "is due to circumstances over which he really had no control." The expression is not particularly menacing, but a warning of a rather difficult nature. All lamoids tend to be quarrelsome, spitting when they are angry—habits which they share with camels.

There is a story about a vicuña which illustrates the bad-tempered characteristics of these animals. Some years ago one of these animals was taken to Machu Picchu and released to graze on the terraces so as to provide an added feature of interest for visitors. For some reason it developed a peculiar dislike for ladies, and would rush up to them in a threatening way, sometimes biting and even spitting. Its attentions became such an embarrassment that it had to be removed, banished to the mountains, and was then replaced by a more docile alpaca.

Besides having difficult natures, camels and llamas share a number of features which have enabled zoologists to place them in the same family. They belong to a group of large mammals (the class of animals which feed their young with milk) that are herbivorous. Their stomach is remarkable in having three compartments or pouches. As they graze or browse, food is stored in the first of these compartments. Later, when the animals are resting, the food is regurgitated and then chewed leisurely and thoroughly—a process known as "chewing the cud."

As members of a further group known as the Cloven-hoofed mammals, camels and their relatives walk on two toes; the underside of the foot, in other words, is divided by a cleft or deep furrow. Additionally, in the camel family, the main part of the foot is converted to a pair of tough padded soles, which are very suitable for walking on sandy or slippery rock surfaces.

10

In lamoids, the underside of the foot, behind the nails, is made up of a pair of tough elastic pads or cushions.

Animals with this special kind of foot form a side-group of the hoofed animals called the Tylopoda (from the Greek, meaning "cushion-footed"). Camels and lamoids are the only surviving representatives of this group.

In the distant past there were many other kinds of tylopods. They flourished in the great grasslands of western North America, where they must have been spectacular beasts during the Tertiary period twenty to forty million years ago. Megatylops was a long-necked giant, fifteen feet tall, and among the largest of the plains animals of its day. By the end of the great Ice Age of the Pleistocene these early tylopods had died out in North America—but not before some had migrated into northern Asia and South America.

The story of the tylopods, pieced together from fossil records, is a fascinating one. It illustrates the great conflicts and migrations that must have occurred in the past. It also tells us something about how our continents became linked.

North and South America are joined by a neck of land known as Central America. Until a few million years ago, however, this land connection did not exist. Where it now lies there was a string of volcanic islands, and the southern boundary of North America lay somewhere in Mexico. South America was beyond the sea to the south, a great island continent of its own.

The connection between North and South America followed violent movements of the Earth's crust some five million years ago. New land was heaved upward to bridge a number of the islands and so form the land connection of Central America. As soon as this corridor was established an interchange of animals took place. Deer, tapirs, bears, peccaries, and lamoids moved southward, while others, such as opossums and armadillos, went in the opposite direction.

The ancestral camels, in their turn, strayed northward and westward along a strip of land now submerged beneath the Bering Sea. Their descendants are the dromedary, a domestic animal of the dry regions of northern Africa and southern Asia, and the two-humped Bactrian camel which survives in the wild in the Gobi Desert of Mongolia. For some unknown reason their relatives remaining in North America dwindled in numbers and finally disappeared.

The Bering Strait land bridge brought another important wave of immigrants. At a time now believed to be around 25,000 B.C., a branch of the human race known as Mongoloids crossed to the east to become the ancestors of the American Indians. The first of these nomadic people followed the lamoids into South America some 15,000 to 20,000 years ago.

The lamoids by that time had spread throughout much of South America. We know that early types of llama lived in the broad plains of the north of Argentina, and later vanished. An animal like the vicuña also lived there. Eventually, two types became more successful than the others, and these gave rise to the vicuña and to the guanaco.

The first men to reach the Andes would have seen both these lamoids. The smaller, fleet-footed vicuña lived in the central parts of the mountains where it was drier. Its relative, the guanaco, had a similar range in the north, but in the south it

12

spread beyond the Andes, crossing the bleak plains of Patagonia to the very tip of the continent. Bands of nomadic hunters followed the herds of guanaco, themselves reaching the Strait of Magellan about 10,000 years ago. Descendants of these people, the Fuegian and Patagonian Indians, and the Huarpes of the San Juan region of Argentina, depended upon the herds of guanaco for their livelihood. These animals were as important to them as seals were to the Eskimo and bison to the North American Indians.

The origin of the llama and alpaca is an interesting puzzle, for neither exists in the wild. Most probably both were derived from the guanaco, and certain characteristics of the teeth and skull support this belief. Native peoples have long been in the habit of keeping young guanacos as pets, so it is not difficult to see how these changes came about. As man's slaves, they gradually evolved from their original form. Early herdsmen, by selecting the offspring they preferred and keeping them apart, improved the wild stock—just as fine breeds of sheep and cattle have been raised in our own times. One kind, the llama, was kept for its ability to carry loads, and another, the alpaca, gave its masters wool. These pre-Inca herders may not have been the first to select and raise animals in this way (sheep and goats were probably domesticated earlier in the Old World), but they were the first to do so in the Americas.

All known evidence suggests that Andean man and the llama came together at an early period—at least four thousand years ago. Remains of sacrificed llamas have been found at an ancient pre-Inca temple site in Peru. Near Humahuaca, in northwestern Argentina, there is a cave known as the Gruta del Inca. Rock paintings in this cave depict a line of lamoids joined together by a rope, which suggests that they were domesticated. Unfortunately, no precise date can be given to these paintings, but Argentinean experts believe them to be very old. One curious

Cave paintings of lamoids and ostrichlike rheas in the Gruta del Inca, northwestern Argentina

feature is that some of the animals have a ruff of long hairs at the base of the neck, which is characteristic of the vicuña.

Another theory for the origin of the llama and the alpaca infers that they came, not from the guanaco, but from some now extinct lamoid which lingered on from an earlier era. This animal had long hairlike wool, and a group of these unusual animals was taken into captivity by early nomadic Indians. It is thought that the wild animals then died out, possibly with changing climatic conditions, leaving only the captive ones which gave rise to the domestic types of today.

Whatever the background of the llama and alpaca, their domestication brought great changes to the life of the Indians. By the time Europe entered the Christian era, communities had settled in the highlands of the central Andes. They cultivated a variety of food crops, they wore warm woolen clothes, and they drove teams of llamas to carry their produce and belongings. In other words, they were sufficiently advanced to be able to devote some of their time to leisure activities, to practice and to develop new skills. From these simple yet necessary beginnings there grew the great civilization that was to impose its will over a vast region of the Andes.

Frequently in this book I shall refer to the Incas, the Quechua-speaking peoples (who lived originally around Cuzco in Peru) and to the empire over which they ruled. It was these peoples who, under their hereditary leaders, conquered lands stretching for 2,500 miles; this they did without the help or knowledge of wheeled transport. Instead, they employed llamas in tens of thousands to carry supplies to the distant outposts of their empire—a remarkable achievement unparalleled in history.

Pen-and-ink drawing, made around the end of the sixteenth century, showing Indians and a pack llama under their Spanish overseer.

Pack llamas are used for carrying produce to and from highland markets of the central Andes. Shorter legs and longer wool of the neck distinguish the domestic llama from the guanaco.

Man and beast alike have to be adapted to live at high elevations in the Andes. The alpaca and the vicuña seldom if ever come below 12,000 feet, and the llama thrives best at altitudes above 8,000 feet. The thin air at these heights allows great changes in temperature, with a range of 70° in a day by no means rare. When the sun shines it is scorchingly hot, but the moment it is obscured by cloud, or when night falls, heat is lost very rapidly. The thick fleeces of the lamoids, which trap protective layers of air, are ideal to blanket the effects of these changes. Another great strain is imposed by the low oxygen content of the atmosphere. At 18,000 feet (which is near the upper limit of life in the Andes) there is only half as much life-giving oxygen as there is at sea level. So, an animal's lungs have to have an increased capacity, and the oxygenated blood has to be pumped more efficiently around the body—otherwise the unpleasant symptoms of mountain sickness are experienced. Both lamoids and Andean Indians have enlarged lungs, big hearts, and a vastly increased number of red blood cells.

To be able to develop and thrive in the Andes called for these body changes, or adaptations. Even though the lamoids were very successful it is only in the wild and high places that we may see them today. The vicuña is rare, restricted to areas where it is protected or out of reach of man; it has had a tragic history linked with the lives and fortunes of the Incas. Alpacas graze their traditional pasturelands, beneath bright skies and towering snow-capped peaks, much as they have done for centuries. There, too, striding softly along the narrow stony ways of the Peruvian and Bolivian mountains will be found llamas, carrying food and merchandise for the Indians. Two thousand miles away, on the plains of Patagonia and haunting the forest fringes of Tierra del Fuego, are the largest guanaco herds still in existence. Theirs is a bleak land, facing the Antarctic seas and swept by icy winds in winter.

This, then, is the world of the lamoids, whose life story we shall be tracing in this book.

The guanaco is the widest ranging of the lamoids and South America's tallest animal. In Argentina, the male leader of a family group is called the relincho, *meaning "neigh"—from its shrill call.*

2. Daughters of the Yellow Sand

The name *guanaco* goes far back into antiquity. It comes from Quechua, the ancient language of Peru, which has also given us the words *llama, alpaca,* and *vicuña.* The guanaco, however, was widely known to early peoples in South America, and throughout its range had many different names. One of the more charming and descriptive of these was that given by the Ona Indians of Tierra del Fuego, who spoke of these wild llamas as "Daughters of the Yellow Sand."

Guanacos are fond of rolling in soft, sandy soil. This helps to keep their fleeces in trim and to relieve skin irritations. But the Onas believed that it was responsible for the yellowish brown coloring which extends over their back, sides, and shoulders. It is a rich color, fading to white underneath and to smoky gray on the face and forehead, while the stubby tail is chocolate brown. These contrasting hues give the guanaco a handsome and striking appearance.

The male stands a little over six feet high—rather more than the female—and is the tallest of South America's wild animals. The height is exaggerated by the long neck and legs, for the body is about the size of a large deer. When startled, a guanaco plunges and dips its neck in a way that is very characteristic of the camels; but, normally, relaxed or alert, the head is held high on the gracefully curved neck.

The guanaco has the widest range of the lamoids. It is found in the Andes from Peru to the southern tip of the continent; eastward it extends across to the province of Buenos Aires, and from there roams southward throughout much of Patagonia. Across the Strait of Magellan, it is on Isla Grande and on the Chilean island of Navarino—places which it probably reached by swimming or by crossing over on ice during an exceptionally severe winter. Its altitude range extends from sea level to 17,000 feet.

Guanacos vary slightly from place to place. Those of the north (of the Peruvian Andes) are smaller than Patagonian animals, and the two are regarded as distinct kinds or races. The guanacos of Isla Grande (where the Ona Indians lived) are yellowish brown in color; while those of Navarino and the Patagonian mainland have russet coats with long winter "over-hairs." The Navarino animals are also the largest and heaviest, with the widest feet—which provide a better foothold on the wet spongy moorlands of that island.

Because of hunting, the spread of domestic animals, and other forms of disturbance, the guanaco has now disappeared from many of its old haunts. It is rare today in the wild except in Isla Grande and in remote areas of the dry Patagonian steppe. This steppeland, the southernmost part of the Argentinean mainland, stretches for a thousand miles as a mostly gray, thorny waste, divided by a few river courses that carve a way across from the Andes to the Atlantic Ocean. Sharing this desolate region with the guanacos are sheep, ostrichlike rheas, armadillos, foxes, and several peculiar kinds of rodents such as mara, vizcacha, and tucotuco.

All these animals are adapted in one way or another to resist cold as well as prolonged dry periods. The thick woolly hair of the guanaco provides warmth and insulation against temperatures that fall below freezing in winter. Food may be very scarce, and the herds may travel far in search of soft-leaved grasses and herbs. When these favorite plants are not available, guanacos browse like goats, picking out the shoots of such spiny bushes as the *quilimbai* and *jarilla*. In Tierra del Fuego, herds often move to the coasts in winter and feed on the stout evergreen leaves of *Maytenus*, a shrub related to the climbing bittersweet.

Guanacos live in arid country, but they require water. Whenever possible they spend the night near a spring or waterhole so that they can drink at dawn; afterward, they scatter to graze. The problem of finding enough to drink can be very acute in winter, and in hard times the animals gather in large numbers in the vicinity of any watering place that remains unfrozen.

Guanacos are social animals and normally live in herds. These herds are of two kinds: the *family band*, which has a single male leader, and the *troop*, which is mainly composed of unattached or bachelor males. The band and the troop differ in size, in behavior, and, to some extent, in the places they frequent.

A family band numbers from about five to fifteen animals. These are made up of females and young, together with one male who is their guide and protector. One of his duties is to lead the band when it is on the move; another is to act as rear guard when they are running away from danger. Guanacos are cautious animals and always approach new feeding grounds warily. In hilly country the male normally takes up a position above the others; on flatter ground he makes for any small rise and from it carefully spies out the land before the march continues.

The greatest possible care is taken when the herd is drinking, for enemies often lurk near watering places. The animals approach slowly, ears pricked, eyes and noses alert. The adult male drinks first. When they have all had their fill, the herd moves away, again slowly and anxiously. If sheep or horses are present then they drink first, the guanacos quietly waiting their turn. The presence of other animals generally makes them more

Guanacos await their turn at a drinking pool in the steppeland of eastern Patagonia. Short tails are usually carried arched like a jug handle.

nervous, and they prefer to drink alone at the quietest times and places.

Guanacos like to rest after feeding and during the hot midday hours of the Patagonian summer. To this end a secluded spot is chosen, often in a little depression where they can roll and refresh themselves in the soft soil. They indulge in this activity in the same way as we might enjoy the luxury of a hot bath. White undersides to the sky, they roll and twist and squirm, dust rising into the air. A number of these wallows may be found together, and the scene on a warm day brings to mind tourists idling on a favorite beach. Yet, even at such apparently carefree moments, one animal is on watch, acting as sentinel for the herd.

22

For much of the year guanacos tend to occupy a familiar territory. A defined home range has the advantage of spacing out the animals and so ensures even supplies of food; this is particularly important when the young are born. The range also provides a fixed area where the leader can more easily guard and keep his herd together.

Fights between rival males, although seldom prolonged, are violent and bad-tempered. The first signs of conflict occur when a strange male approaches a band, perhaps trotting forward defiantly, with neck and head high. A closer look at his adversary may make him change his mind, in which case he turns and a conflict is avoided. On these occasions the leader may chase the stranger for a short distance, before returning to his band.

If the rival is more determined, then a serious contest ensues. At first, the animals come together with a weaving and clashing of necks as each tries to incapacitate the other. Knees bang and a cloud of dust envelops the combatants. With squealing, biting, and kicking, the fight then becomes more angry. Forefeet are used to strike downward, and if one animal is knocked down or brought to its knees then the other quickly has an advantage. Teeth wounds and torn ears are the results of these sharp encounters. Fortunately, it is soon over, the vanquished retires, dust settles, and peace is restored.

If a contest has been evenly matched, the victor may have little energy left to chase his rival; instead, he stays with the band and licks his wounds. The established leader of a band usually fights to the last of his resources. Whatever the result, the defeated animal moves away to a solitary life, possibly, in time, to join an all-male troop. A young male, overthrown in a struggle, may go in search of another band with a weaker leader. Thus it is the strongest males that breed and so continue the race.

Young guanacos, known in Patagonia as *chulengos*, are born

Chulengos are delightful creatures, resembling small Bambis, with longer, more elegant, and more beautiful necks.

in the spring and early summer, that is, between October and December. In the Peruvian Andes seasons are less well marked, and the young there appear from April to June, at a time when the best pasture is available. Usually one young is produced at a time.

Chulengos are delightful creatures, resembling small Bambis, with longer, more elegant, and more beautiful necks. Their coats are pale at first and very soft and silky. They can run almost as soon as they are born, but for a day or two are a little knock-kneed and unsteady. However, very soon they can keep up with their mothers, trotting along by her side on long slender legs. From her they learn to smell the winds, to choose their foods, and to explore the land. Guanacos make model mothers, nursing and keeping a watchful eye on their young for many months. When the time comes for them to leave, male chulengos go to a troop, thus beginning an independent life.

Young females, too, may leave when their mothers cease nursing them, eventually to join another band.

By contrast to the family band, the troop is an open society whose members are free to come and go as they please. It is generally larger, more constantly on the move, and less well disciplined. It is composed of immature males, mostly yearlings and two-year-olds, who have been joined perhaps by a few elderly animals; sometimes fifty or more join forces in this way. In the past, when guanacos were more abundant, much larger troops existed. Captain John Wood, a seventeenth-century English navigator, wrote of seeing herds of "Winnackews or Spanish sheep" six or seven hundred strong in Patagonia.

The troop has no leader and its members behave more or less as a group. The larger the concentration of animals the more they need to roam in search of fresh pastures—often frequenting very wild country, such as mountain foothills and the borders of the steppe. The weakness of the troop lies in the fact that it has no leader and in a surprise attack may be thrown into disorder. But its members enjoy one great advantage through being together, that is, the benefit of increased vigilance. Everyone takes a turn as lookout, and it is very difficult for a predator to creep up without being detected. At the first sign of danger, a shrill neigh of alarm is given, and the whole troop is on the alert.

Individuals can never be so watchful and consequently they run greater risks. Sad to say, the days of a lone guanaco are usually numbered. The most feared enemy is the night-hunting puma, or mountain lion. Guanacos reduce the chances of being surprised by one of these large cats by gathering together and sleeping in the open. On the plains, in moments of sudden danger, they have been seen to bunch into a circle with the older animals on the outside—a tactic which may deter young and inexperienced predators. Although they are very capable

25

of using their feet and teeth if cornered, the main defense of the guanaco lies in flight.

For a large plains animal it is not particularly fast, galloping at a top speed of about thirty-five miles per hour. But it moves with an easy, loose-limbed grace, maintaining this speed over long distances, and hardly slackening over rough and broken country. Usually, well-worn trails are followed, but these are abandoned if an attacker is close. Sometimes, a leader and members of his band separate and go in different directions. The leader chooses steep or difficult places, clearing fences and stream beds with a single bound, and leaving pursuers—particularly if they are men on horseback and dogs—far behind. Meanwhile, the others, under the temporary leadership of an old female, move to a safer spot to await the return of their master.

Guanacos are good swimmers. This explains their presence on islets off the coast of the Valdés Peninsula in Patagonia where they were seen by Charles Darwin in 1833. In Tierra del Fuego it has been narrated how the Indians there hunted them in wintertime with packs of dogs. If the guanacos were prevented by snow from escaping into the mountains, then they took to the water. The Indians, in canoes, were ready for this and quickly overtook the tired animals.

Although normally cautious animals, guanacos have an irrepressible curiosity. They gaze intently at anything new in their territory, sometimes even following a person for a considerable distance. An incident a few years ago in Tierra del Fuego first drew my attention to this strange aspect of their behavior.

On a blustery March day a companion and I were taken in a light airplane to a deserted spot in the south of Isla Grande, not far from the Beagle Channel. We had traveled to that part of the island expressly to see guanacos, for they have a stronghold there, now that the Ona Indians have gone and sheep farmers

26

Charles Darwin noticed that guanacos readily take to the water, several times watching them swimming between these islands at Port Valdés on the Atlantic coast of Patagonia.

are generally content not to molest them. From the landing strip we made our way inland, carrying food and warm clothing for several days. Soon we were weaving our way through a forest of tangled trees and branches, heading for the mountains.

These mountains are the southernmost ramparts of the great range of the Andes. They are not high compared with peaks farther north, but at this latitude they are seldom free of snow. At a little over a thousand feet, the forest gives way to a dense scrub of antarctic beech and beyond this rises open, swampy moorland. Our first signs of guanacos were at this upper edge of the forest. Winding through the scrub were well-trodden trails, made by the animals as they moved between higher and lower ground with the changing seasons. We were glad of these ready-made paths which helped us considerably with our own walking. The next day, in a freezing mist, we crossed a pass and descended into a long wooded valley. Moving ahead of us, in the distance, we saw a line of guanacos, soon to disappear

over a ridge. A single animal lingered for a moment behind the others, silhouetted against the sky. That evening we came to a lake and, later, sitting by a campfire, the mist rising above the forest, a guanaco called from the slopes above.

It was a strange, eerie call, which I can best describe as a kind of whinny—much as you might expect an asthmatic horse to make. Nearer and nearer it came. Finally, after long moments, a pale form emerged from the shadows, stepping lightly between the lichen-draped trees. Alert and graceful, its upright ears edged with white, it stood very close to us—a wonderful sight in the silvered twilight of that Fuegian forest.

We were now long and intently surveyed by the guanaco. Presently, it began to move, slowly and deliberately, ears and eyes still turned to us. Several times it seemed about to go back into the forest, but lingered for another gaze. I supposed it to be the leader of a band whose companions were waiting quietly nearby. No doubt he was disturbed at finding something new in his territory, and one could sense uncertainty in his manner. Dangers, it might be thought, are never quite so bad if they can be kept in sight! But what seemed so strange was that he deliberately called attention to himself by sudden movements and by the weird noises which he continued to utter from time to time. Possibly our stillness baffled him, and had we been identifiable at the outset he would have been content with less provoking behavior. At length, as suddenly as he had appeared, he melted into the forest, sending back a hoarse chuckle out of the darkness.

Many travelers have written about the strange antics of guanacos. They have been seen running up and down hillsides, for no apparent reason. In the mountains of Tierra del Fuego, Darwin watched a guanaco which not only neighed and squealed when he approached but pranced about in a very odd way, almost as if it were challenging him. Elsewhere, one was witnessed chasing a fox, both animals twisting and turning as if they were enjoying a game. Guanacos, with their playful and unpredictable ways, are always fascinating animals to watch.

Perhaps one of the strangest things about them is the story of their having regular places to die. In the past it was believed that these were traditional sites to which old and infirm animals went when they felt their days were ended. These dying places, or cemeteries as they have been called, have been found in the Patagonian steppes and in the open grasslands of northern Tierra del Fuego. The Anglo-Argentinean naturalist W. H. Hudson wrote on this subject and suggested the most probable explanation. Large accumulations of guanaco bones have always been found in thickets and places that are protected in some way from the weather. Such spots, which are few and far between in these desolate regions, are likely to be remembered as places of refuge, and so to one of these a sick animal tries to go, there very possibly to die. Guanacos, too, tend to congregate in winter, when drifting snow and shortage of food can cause the deaths of many animals at the same time. This legend is a sad note on which to end a chapter, but it does conjure up a picture of the chill southern lands which are the guanaco's main home today.

3. Nomads of the Plains

Not long ago I was walking with a friend among some sand dunes on the coast of the Valdés Peninsula in Patagonia. He picked up a curious rounded stone and remarked that it had been fashioned by the Indians. It was smooth, about the size of a baseball, and had a neat groove around the middle. Quite frequently, he said, broken pieces were found, but a smoothly rounded surface gave them away as parts of some primitive implement. They were made by the nomadic Tehuelche Indians and were weights for a weapon known as *boleadoras* or bolas, that they used for hunting guanacos.

Three stones were used in each set of bolas (others with two weights were for hunting rheas). Two of these weights were heavy, while the third was rather lighter and more elongated. All three were encased in leather and joined by long, twisted strips of skin. The hunter held the lightest of the three weights in his hand, whirled the bolas like a lasso, and then released it at the guanaco being hunted. If he aimed well the leather thongs with their heavy weights wound round the long legs or neck of the animal and prevented it from escaping, and then the Indian or his companion quickly ran up to kill the victim.

The Tehuelches were the original inhabitants of the plains of Patagonia. Their territory extended from the river Negro to the Strait of Magellan, and from the Andes in the west to the Atlantic coast. The few early photographs that exist show these

Indians dressed in loose robes, conical-shaped hats, and foot-wear made from the skins of guanacos. Their homes were branch frames covered with hides. As well as bolas, they used bows and arrows for hunting. Arrowheads were made from stone, chipped and serrated to the sharpness of a knife edge; for a bowstring they used a piece of sinew from the leg of a guanaco. The livelihood of these people entirely depended upon the herds they hunted.

By the eighteenth century the Tehuelches had acquired horses—brought originally to South America by settlers from Europe. The Indians soon became expert riders, hunting guanacos on horseback with bolas and spears. By that time a war had begun to wage with the new settlers over the ownership of land. The elusive Tehuelches on their swift steeds proved

Left: Monotonous scrubland of the Patagonian steppe—former home of the nomadic, guanaco-hunting Tehuelche Indians.

Below: The Tehuelche toldo, or tent, was made from guanaco skins sewn together and fitted over a framework of poles. The open side normally faced eastward—away from the prevailing winds. Inside were arranged sleeping compartments, separated from one another by skin partitions.

formidable adversaries, raiding settlements in the isolated valleys and then disappearing into the trackless steppe. But the struggle was one-sided, and by the end of the last century the Indians had been finally defeated and vanished forever from their old haunts. Their disappearance left the way open for the growth of the great sheep-raising *estancias* for which Patagonia is now famous.

Before we trace the history of the guanaco through these years, it is interesting to say more about these nomadic Indians. The first time they were seen by Europeans was during the voyage of Ferdinand Magellan. His fleet spent the winter of 1520 near San Julián on the coast of Patagonia, where the Indians were in the habit of coming down to the shore. Their moccasined feet, padded with dry grasses for warmth, greatly impressed the European sailors who called the Tehuelches *Patagones*—men with big feet. In the official account of the voyage, Antonio Pigafetta also described the guanaco. He wrote, these giant men were clothed in the skins of a beast "that had a large head, ears like a mule, the body of a camel, and tail of a horse." These animals were then very common in the land.

The Tehuelches were tireless and skillful hunters. They could learn a great deal from the tracks of a herd left in the soft sandy soil of the plains. From these they knew how many males and how many females were present, roughly the size of each animal, how long since the herd had passed, and if the animals were in a frightened or nervous state. An important time of the year for the Tehuelches was the spring and early summer when the chulengos were born, for their fleeces made the softest and warmest of their garments. Sadly, and cruelly to our minds, the young guanacos were hunted before they were more than a day or two old. Pelts were pulled from the tiny bodies and put out to dry by the Indians' tents. Similarly, strips of flesh were hung to dry, for this was a time of abundance and festivity.

34

Nineteenth-century engraving showing a Tehuelche hunting scene. Whirling their bolas, the circle of riders charges a guanaco herd while one Indian dismounts to kill a rhea. Pumas are also disturbed with the frightened animals.

Guanaco hunts during the nineteenth century, of which there are several first-hand accounts, seem to have been wild and reckless affairs. To the Tehuelche Indian, a man's standing was judged by his ability in the chase. He rode off with a companion, each man taking with him two horses and his dogs. A number of these groups formed an immense circle into the center of which game would be driven. They scoured a large area of countryside, maintaining contact meanwhile with smoke signals. Gradually the riders drew closer, driving frightened animals before them. Then at a given moment, the men mounted their led horses and, whirling their bolas above their heads, charged into the frantic herds from all sides. It is not difficult to imagine the noise, the dust, and the confusion. The dogs too took part in the terrible chase which left dead and dying guanacos, rheas, and other game scattered over the plain.

35

The Ona Indians stalked guanacos among the rolling Fuegian forests of southern beech.

The Onas, who were related to the Tehuelches, did not indulge in these wild escapades. For one thing, they never had horses, and it is not certain that they knew anything about the technique of using bolas. Furthermore, their country—or a large part of it—did not lend itself in the same way to a great roundup. Much of the Isla Grande is covered with rolling forests of southern beech, and in the south are the mountains. The land is more humid, temperatures are less extreme, and there is no periodic shortage of food for the guanacos. Consequently, the animals tend to have more or less fixed territories, although in winter they move down to the coasts and valleys.

The Onas were never a large tribe. In early times they probably numbered no more than two or three thousand, spread across an island about the size of the state of West Virginia. Their lives were of the utmost simplicity. As a protection against the wind and cold they made themselves lean-to shelters of branches and hides. The men wore robes made from a pair of guanaco skins stitched together with sinews. Unlike the Tehuelches, the Onas wore their robes with the hair on the outside —perhaps not so warm as having it on the inside, but it provided a good disguise and gave better protection against rain. The garment hung loosely with the right arm usually left free. The women's mantles were similar, but shorter. The traditional headdress was a triangular piece of gray skin taken from the forehead of a guanaco.

Hunting in the forests of Tierra del Fuego required special

An early photograph of Ona Indians, former inhabitants of Isla Grande in Tierra del Fuego. Guanaco skins were worn with the hair on the outside, thus providing the hunters with a good disguise when stalking their quarry.

skills. Sometimes a number of Onas hunted together, encircling their prey. At other times, a man hunted on his own. The Indians stalked with great care, treading cautiously among the many fallen branches and paying attention to the slope of the land, for guanacos tend to make for high ground when they are frightened. Suitably disguised, a hunter approached his prey, blending with the pale lichens on the trees. When he had maneuvered close to a herd, he slipped on a bowstring (which was kept dry until the last possible moment), then, stepping lightly out of his heavy robe, he edged forward to place an arrow, if possible, just behind the ribs of the guanaco he had selected. If he shot well—as the animal turned from him—then the sharp stone-tipped arrow quickly found its mark. But if the animal was only wounded, a long chase might follow, until his quarry had weakened and the hunter could come near enough to place the final shot. After the kill, the Indian would go back to retrieve any precious arrows that he had lost on the way.

The body was skinned and normally divided into six portions to be carried back to camp. Little was wasted—skin, bones, and sinews all had a use in the Ona household. Although these early Fuegians hunted other animals, their livelihood, like that of the Tehuelches, depended upon the guanaco.

The guanaco was also important to other peoples. These included the Puelches of northern Patagonia and the Argentinean Pampa; the Querandí (another Pampa tribe); a group of the fierce Araucanian Indians; and the Huarpe Indians, who lived near present-day Mendoza in Argentina. The Huarpes, mentioned earlier, are of special interest because their way of hunting guanacos had similarities with the great annual hunt, or *chaco*, of the Incas. In mountainous areas, many of the Indians gathered together to drive the animals into a narrow gorge or valley where they could be attacked on both sides with bolas and arrows. Many animals would be killed as a result of these

Competing with sheep for the sparse pasture, guanacos have now been driven into the wilder and more remote parts of Patagonia.

great sweeps through the countryside. In flatter areas, several Indians might take part in a simple chase, one man taking over from another until their victim fell exhausted.

The arrival of European settlers brought many changes to the plains of Patagonia. Nomadic Indians disappeared, land was fenced, and flocks of sheep grazed the choicest pastures. All these had an effect on the guanacos. Perhaps the most surprising thing is that their numbers actually increased at first. The slow-moving sheep provided easy prey for pumas, and they consequently deserted the guanacos for this new fare. Shepherds then had to hunt the large cats and in so doing they removed a natural check on the guanacos. So their herds thrived and within a few years of settlement they were probably more abundant than they had been during aboriginal days.

Quite soon the sheep farmers realized that the wild lamoids

39

competed with their own animals for food. One guanaco, they calculated, ate as much as three or four sheep. What was more disturbing was the belief that some of the diseases they carried could be transferred to sheep. The settlers therefore tried to restore the balance, not so much by killing adult guanacos as by hunting the young, whose skins had a market value. So the killing of chulengos again became fashionable, and a trade developed supplying merchants with the soft pelts. So ruthless were the hunters that in many places hardly a chulengo survived. The adults were of little interest, for they were harder to catch, and their meat and hides anyway were of inferior quality. The traders eventually drove themselves out of business, and in the process the herds of guanaco were brought to a very sorry state. Few young animals had grown up to bolster their numbers and, while to a casual observer they appeared to be in no immediate danger, they were soon to vanish from many parts of the plains. The same thing was happening elsewhere. Farther north in Argentina, and in the mountains of the central Andes, the great herds that had been seen by the early Spaniards no longer existed. Their decline, too, had been due to man and excessive hunting.

4. Vicuña of the High Andes

The silken-haired vicuña, smallest of the lamoids, lives in the high treeless region of the central Andes. Its home is among the bleak and rather dry uplands, called *punas*, which stretch between the upper limits of the forest or cultivation and the line of permanent snows—an elevation between about 12,000 and 16,500 feet. Much of this land is covered with coarse bunch grasses, with here and there gentle valleys and moist depressions where the vegetation is greener. It is in the upper part of the punas, above the traditional grazing lands of alpacas, where one may hope to find the vicuñas.

When it was first seen by Europeans in the sixteenth century, the vicuña was plentifully distributed throughout the greater part of the kingdom of the Incas. Today it is confined to a narrow 1,300-mile range stretching from the south of Peru to the province of San Juan in Argentina, and even there it is far from common, with its populations no longer linked. In between are great areas where there are no vicuñas, where grazing by domestic animals and other disturbances have made conditions unsuitable for them. In Bolivia, for example, small groups survive on either side of the great lake of Titicaca, and there are other groups scattered along the borders with Chile. In Chile itself the vicuña inhabits parts of the mountain fringes of the Atacama Desert, a desolate but beautiful region set among some of the loftiest peaks of the Andes.

Despite the animal's scarcity and the inhospitable nature of the punas, it is not difficult to reach parts of vicuña-land. In Peru and northern Chile a number of motor roads wind inland into the bare hills, and in the space of a few hours one can travel from the warm shores of the Pacific to cool Andean heights. Several times I have made such a journey and before the end of the day seen vicuñas. The first of these memorable journeys was in the mountains of northern Chile.

One hot day I drove inland from the coast near Arica, along a road that twisted and climbed as a black ribbon amid fantastic desert scenery. Towering ridges succeeded deep crumbling

The vicuña inhabits high rolling grasslands, or punas, of the central Andes. Typical vegetation is wiry grasses, of several species, called ichu *by the Indians. Elsewhere grow evergreen* tola *shrubs (belonging to the daisy family) and hard cushion plants.*

valleys, and the parched land seemed drained of all life and color. With some relief, late in the afternoon, I emerged onto a broad grassy plateau which ran across to distant snow-capped mountains. The road continued uncertainly, and my car slid in and out of ruts left by previous vehicles. Moving on, uncomfortably aware of the growing coldness of night at an altitude of 14,000 feet, I began to wonder if I would reach my destination of Parinacota that evening. Suddenly, close by the road, I noticed a group of five vicuñas.

It was the perfect setting in which to see them, against mountains gilded by the honeyed light of evening. I had not seen

A pale face and ruff of long hairs falling below the neck distinguish the vicuña from the guanaco. The animals also have wonderfully soft and silky fleeces which help them tolerate rapid temperature changes, from scorching heat during the day to sudden cold at night.

vicuñas before and I carefully studied their pale faces, white and golden tawny coats, and the delicate mane of long hairs which fell below their slender necks. Their grace and poise reminded me of antelopes rather than of their close relative, the guanaco. After a long gaze they moved away, slowly at first, then breaking into a gallop, their hoofs putting up wispy plumes of dust that hung on the air like Indian smoke signals.

Parinacota (meaning "flamingo-lake"), which I reached after dusk, is a settlement of low thatched houses clustered around an old church. It is the home of Aymará alpaca herders who graze their herds around several broad shallow lakes near the village. Each evening the animals are brought to the safety of stone-walled enclosures near the Indians' homes. At 14,800 feet it is too high to cultivate crops, and, except when the sun is shining, it is a cold cheerless place. During the several days I spent there the herders told me about the vicuñas.

There were two to three hundred in the nearby mountains. They kept away from the domestic flocks, preferring to be alone on the higher and quieter slopes. Vicuñas rise with the sun, or rather later in cloudy weather, leaving their overnight resting places on some dry protected hillside. They then set off to drink and to search for soft grasses and herbs growing by streams and in marshy places. On better-drained slopes they eat rosettes of squat little plants called *nototriche* and snip the shoots of dwarf evergreen *tola* shrubs. Foraging takes up the greater part of their day.

So alert and shy were the vicuñas near Parinacota that I only saw them again in the distance. Their nervousness was largely due to dogs of the Indian herders which often worried them. Usually they make for higher ground when disturbed, galloping with boundless ease in the thin mountain air. With ears held

Alpaca herders' homes at Parinacota, high in the Andes of northern Chile

sharply back and the head kept on an even course by the long supple neck, they cover broken and slippery ground with an amazing speed. Gullies are negotiated along well-remembered trails, the animals clambering down and reappearing on the far side with a magical ease that baffles pursuers.

Research in recent years by scientists concerned for the vicuña's future has given us much information about the little lamoid's day-to-day life and behavior. Like guanacos, they live in family parties or bands and bachelor troops; in addition one comes across solitary males.

Life in the band is regulated by an adult male who, year round, maintains a territory against rivals. Whenever another male approaches, he gallops to the boundary of his territory and stands there stiffly erect with head and tail high. By standing, so to speak, on tiptoes, he tries to make himself appear as tall as possible in a way intended to frighten his rival. Very often the ruse succeeds, for a healthy male vicuña is practically invincible in his own territory. If a whole troop appears then he chases one or two of the intruders, making high trilling screeches, which usually have the effect of putting the rest to flight. A defeated animal always shows submission by lowering its head and tail and depressing its ears. Encounters between male vicuñas, however, are usually limited to aggressive display and pursuit.

Carl Koford, who made a long study of the vicuña, found that males (unlike some other territorial animals) do not prevent females from leaving their band. But neighboring females may be attacked if they come too close—in the same way as rival males. A female, in fact, prefers to stay in her own band because she knows the home range and because of the likelihood of attack if she strays too far.

Besides reducing actual strife, territories help to space out the vicuña herds. In the most barren parts of their range, such

46

as the great gravel plains near Sabaya and Uyuni in southwestern Bolivia, the territories may be very large—possibly a thousand acres or more being necessary to support one animal. In the best grazing areas, the average density is one animal to about every ten acres. The size of a territory is thus related to the number in the band and availability of food.

Apart from the rare taruca deer, the vicuña has few natural competitors for its food. The largest are the Andean goose and a bushy-tailed rodent called the mountain vizcacha. Its main rivals today are sheep and alpacas, which are forcing vicuñas to go ever higher in their search for pasture.

For some nine months of the year the punas are very dry. This is the so-called winter season of the central Andes, when the country has a drab, yellowish appearance. In December, the rains come and these bring a new cycle of abundance. Flowers suddenly bloom as they do in deserts elsewhere and their drifts of color brighten the land. The weather, for humans, is miserable, but this is the time when the young vicuñas are born.

Like the young of most herbivores, vicuñas can stand almost as soon as they are born. A few days later they are gamboling like lambs, chasing one another and dashing in and out among the adults. A favorite game is for two to stage a duel, facing one another like little fencers, thrusting and wrestling with their slender necks, legs braced on the ground. This so-called "play-fighting" attunes the young combatants for sterner encounters in adult life. Young vicuñas are especially fond of playing in the late afternoon, before they lie down alongside their mothers for the night.

Mother vicuñas look after their offspring until they are about eight months old. Cold winds and frost are the main hazards for the young, despite the parent's care and their own wonderfully soft and silky fleeces. But there are also enemies—besides dogs

47

and men—in that vast and seemingly empty land. Foxes and several kinds of mountain cats roam the punas, and overhead flies the great-winged condor. Maybe more than half of the year's newborn vicuñas will die before they reach an age of six months. It seems tragic, but we must remember that a low rate of survival is necessary if populations are to stay within the limits of the land's resources.

Protection of the band is the responsibility of the adult male. While the females and young are grazing he customarily stands a little apart and keeps guard. The moment danger appears he gives a clear whistling trill and immediately all the others gather near him, craning their necks to see what threatens. In flight, they move cautiously at first, then break into a gallop with the male falling in behind to cover the retreat. If he is separated or killed, the females quickly become confused, thereby increasing their own danger.

In general, vicuña troops are smaller than those of guanacos, rarely more than forty animals ever coming together at one time. Because of grazing pressure and the hostility of territorial males, they tend to frequent drier and less attractive parts of the punas. New recruits from the bands begin to arrive about November. Young of both sexes probably leave the family parties when their mothers cease nursing them, young males to join the bachelor troops and females to go to solitary territorial males or to fresh bands.

Squabbles, involving kicks, bites, and bouts of spitting, are not uncommon within the herds. Vicuñas are nervous and temperamental animals, and such encounters occur among females and juveniles, as well as among troop males. Spitting by lamoids is a sudden forced expulsion of air, carrying with it saliva and particles of masticated food, which is aimed at the face of a victim. When delivering it, the protagonist's ears are laid back, the head and lips are pointed forward, and the ex-

Vicuñas live in high, semiarid country. Their favorite food consists of soft-leaved grasses and herbs which they find in moist depressions and alongside streams.

pression is one of spiteful relish. It is an act of distaste, writes Dr. Koford, "that shows displeasure insufficient to merit a kick."

A remarkable habit of vicuñas and other lamoids is that of depositing their dung at special places. The pellets accumulate in large mounds which often form distinctive features in country occupied by these animals. No doubt these serve as territorial markers, but they also channel excretory chemicals so as to spoil only a small part of the pasturage.

The lives of the vicuña and the guanaco thus bear many resemblances, and from studies of one we are beginning to learn more about the other. But the vicuña lives in a particularly harsh and restricted environment, and in many ways its requirements are more exacting. Its elaborate territorial behavior, low rate of reproduction, and limited size of bands all reflect the problems of survival in the high mountains of the Andes. Ironically, it was the vicuña's ability to live at these altitudes that contributed so significantly to its decline.

5. Royal Hunt of the Incas

The empire of the Incas reached its peak during the fifteenth century. Unknown to the outside world, people throughout a great part of the Andes were ruled with a firm yet benevolent hand from the imperial capital of Cuzco. It was an incredible civilization. All land and property was communally owned, and all work was done for the common good and for the Inca God-king. Fabulous cities, canals, roads, and bridges were built by the toil and endless labor provided by the people. Yet each village and community had to find only such laborers as it could afford to send, and no loyal person was allowed to go hungry. The state was all-powerful and remarkably protective to its people.

The organization of the Incas is all the more significant when we consider the mountainous nature of the land in which they lived. Roads ran to all parts of the empire, but there was no kind of wheeled transport. They had neither wagons nor carts, nor did they have any animals that would have been strong enough to draw vehicles up the steep inclines of their valleys. Instead, alone among the ancient peoples of America, they had pack animals—the sure-footed, slow, and temperamental llama.

Domesticating the llama so as to turn it into a beast of burden must have been a long and tedious task. It has been said, perhaps unkindly, that only the mountain Indian would have had the patience to do it. In any event, the association between

50

man and llama goes back a long way, to the dawn of settled life in the Andes. The Incas' part was to perfect the ancient skills of their predecessors, with the use of alpacas and llamas becoming in due time an integral part of their system of government.

The main task of the pack llamas was to carry state goods and military supplies. Like the Romans, the Incas found that the success of their conquests depended upon regular supplies reaching their garrisons. Regular teams of pack animals traveled the high mountain roads, carrying food, quilted garments, weapons, and other necessities of war. Llama driving was an honored profession, with one man being required on the march for every twelve to fifteen animals. These pack trains were not fast by today's standards, but the llamas were tough; they could endure the cold and long periods without water, and they found their own food. Bones discovered at archaeological sites show that the animals were taken down to the warm valleys of the coast, many doubtless to supply the armies with meat. Huge numbers of animals must have been available for use in those imperial days.

Much has been written about the roads of ancient Peru. These extended for 2,500 miles along the Andes, with branches leading down to the forests on the east and to the coastal valleys on the west. Whenever possible, the roads went straight, breaking into steps on steep slopes. In precipitous places, zigzags and tunnels were cut, and causeways and bridges of several kinds carried men and llamas over marshes and rivers. As all the traffic was on foot, little paving, if any, was needed. On high plains the way was often bounded by walls, which helped to keep pack animals from straying.

Another of the great achievements of the Incas which concerns us here is their mastery of the art of weaving. This also had early beginnings, for warm clothing was a basic necessity for people to be able to develop in the cool highlands of the Andes.

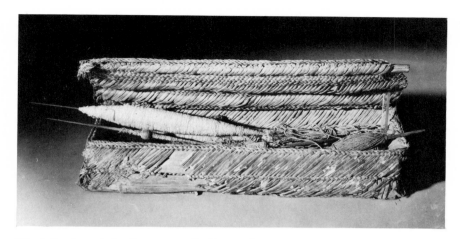

Work basket of the Inca period, above, showing spools of dyed thread for tapestry weaving. Early Peruvian tapestries, woven from alpaca wool, below, are remarkable for their superb symmetry and harmony. Colors are crimson, pink, yellow, black, and white. This fabric was found at Paracas, a dry peninsula on the coast of Peru.

The earliest woven fabrics found in Peru are about four thousand years old. These are small in size and simple in design, suggesting an early stage in the development of this craft. A thousand years later skills had grown enormously, and finds preserved in the deserts alongside cultivated valleys show that the early Peruvians had an amazing knowledge of textiles. They employed a rich variety of techniques for weaving and decorating fabrics—tapestry, twill, brocade, lacelike gauzes, embroidery, and other specialized processes rarely seen today. Some of their finest work has never been equaled from the point of view of skill.

In Inca times the exquisite designs and blending of colors far exceeded day-to-day needs. Richness in clothing was a sign of rank, with the finest and most ornate clothes being worn by members of the royal family. The basic fibers used in early Peruvian garments were cotton, flexible strands from certain plants, and, most predominantly, the wool of lamoids. Llamas and vicuñas, as well as alpacas, supplied wool, each varying in texture and having its different uses.

The coarsest wool used was that of the llama. Normally this was only taken after an animal had become too old for a working life, for males were employed as beasts of burden, and under Inca law it was an offense to kill a healthy female llama. Fleeces, as they became available, were stripped and the wool used for making belts, cords, blankets, and the tough outer garments called ponchos. Hide was cut and fashioned into the soles of sandals, and bone was carved into spoons, needles, spindle whorls, flutes, beads and other ornamental objects.

Alpacas were raised especially for their fine wool, which was used for the clothing of most of the highland people. Like the llamas, they were tended as the communal property of a group of families known as the *ayllu*. In general, the flocks were well segregated according to age, sex, and color. Animals were regularly checked and any found to be suffering from infectious skin diseases had to be killed and buried at once. Each year the *ayllus* sent quotas of wool to public storehouses, where it was set aside for use by the government and the religious institutions of the state. Each family in turn received from the state sufficient wool for its needs.

Apparently, a few alpacas (and llamas) were privately owned in those days. These were most probably acquired as gifts or rewards after some successful military campaign. Wool from such animals added to the allowance that a commoner had already received.

The third and most prized source of wool was the vicuña. These animals were never domesticated, and the wool was collected from wild herds during a great state drive known as the *chaco*. These gatherings took place in each district every three to five years, which gave the vicuña populations a chance to recover before the next hunt. They were important ceremonial occasions, held at the close of the Andean winter.

Much of our information about these royal hunts comes from early accounts made by Spaniards. One of the last to be held in the grand style was in about the year 1534, near the valley of Jauja in Peru, arranged by the Emperor Manco Inca in honor of the Spanish conqueror, Francisco Pizarro. About ten thousand Indians were sent to surround an area of mountains and punas to a circumference of some thirty miles. At a given signal, the huge ring started to close, and with much noise and shouting game was driven in toward the center. Little by little, the men closed ranks until they could join hands. Appointed persons were then sent into the enclosure to kill or capture the animals required by the Emperor.

More than twenty thousand men are said to have taken part in some of the large *chacos*, which lasted several days while whole mountains were searched for game. The conduct of the hunt differed to some extent with the nature of the land. Ideally, the animals would be herded into a narrow valley or ravine, which served as a natural corral. In open country, some kind of enclosure was made, if necessary, by men holding between them woolen threads decorated with feathers and colored streamers. The Swiss naturalist Johann von Tschudi, who watched a vicuña hunt in about 1840, noticed that the timid animals made no attempt to leap over a single strand of rope, being frightened by the pieces of fluttering cloth suspended from it.

The hunt witnessed by von Tschudi, during which 122 animals were captured and killed, was but a shadow of the great *chacos* of former days. Under the eyes of the Incas, ten to fifteen thousand vicuñas might be brought together, with guanacos, deer, foxes, pumas, and perhaps even bears. It must have been an exhilarating spectacle, with the noise and dust, stampeding animals gathering into tight groups, and vicuñas whistling in alarm. Surplus male vicuñas were killed and their fleeces removed. Females of an age to bear young and the strongest-looking males were shorn and released. Probably a number of guanacos and deer were preserved and released in the same way, while harmful animals and any vicuñas that were old or maimed were killed. Counts of all species were taken on *quipus*, the knotted counting strings used by the Incas for keeping records.

Meat obtained during these state hunts was distributed to the people. Each family prepared its own ration, drying and pounding it to make *charqui*, a staple food of the early Peruvians. Altogether, the *chacos* were great festive occasions, designed to secure food for the people as well as to replenish government stocks of wool.

An adult vicuña yields about a third of a pound of wool. In Inca times this was used for making the garments of the Emperor and (according to some historians) members of the nobility. The fine and beautiful weaving was undertaken by chosen handmaidens, the Virgins of the Sun, dedicated to the service of the royal Incas. The Emperor, it is reported, never wore the same clothes twice; there was thus a continuous demand for the fine wool.

An Aymará Indian woman teases and twirls crude wool onto a spindle, while guarding her flock of alpacas (center of picture) and llamas in the highlands of Bolivia.

To make these clothes, wool was first lightly washed and graded according to texture and color. Outer bristles were removed, and the silklike inner hair was then prepared for spinning. Spinning is the process of drawing out the fibers to form a thread. This was done by hand, using the simplest implements: a forked stick, or distaff, for holding the raw wool, and the spindle, which was a narrow rod fitted with a whorl or disc to give it momentum. Fibers from the fluffed and roughly aligned wool on the distaff were teased out, a few at a time, and wound up on the revolving spindle. By retaining the natural oils, the spinner was able to produce a wonderfully silky and pliable thread.

Cloth is woven on a loom. This is a device for holding and interlacing two sets of threads, the weft and the warp. The warp

56

threads are set up on the loom and run the length of the cloth; the weft threads are worked in from side to side lacing the two together. Three basic kinds of looms were used by the early Peruvians. One was an upright frame for making tapestries, at which the weaver worked standing; this type has now disappeared. A second and more important kind was a horizontal backstrap loom, in which tension on two wooden bars holding the warp threads was maintained by stretching them between a stake or tree and a band fastened round the weaver's waist, finished cloth being wound up on the nearest bar as the work progressed. This type of loom is still used by the Aymará Indians of the Bolivian plateau. The maximum width that can be

Backstrap loom of a type still used in the highlands of Bolivia. On such a loom most kinds of fabrics can be made providing the weaver has patience and skill.

A young woman from the Cuzco region working at a curious loom for making a woolen ribbon used for decorating the lower part of women's skirts.

woven on such a loom by a single person is about thirty inches, and the discovery of fabrics up to twenty-seven feet wide was a mystery until it was recalled that women used to work looms in teams, sitting side by side. Some of the finest of all textiles have been woven on these horizontal looms. The third type of loom used was a narrow one for making belts, ribbons, straps, and for tubular seamless articles—in the latter case the warps were fastened to rings instead of loom bars. The way the belt loom was used is shown on a remarkable pottery vessel discovered on the coast of Peru.

Vicuña hairs make the finest and softest woolen threads known for weaving. They are half the width of the finest sheep's wool, and beside them a human hair looks like a piece of coarse wire. Alpaca wool has a greater length and is nearly as fine. Interestingly enough, most, if not all, of the early woolen fabrics found in Peru have been made from alpaca.

The extreme fineness of the spun thread meant that the ancient Peruvian weavers could produce extremely close-textured cloth. Some of the most beautiful of their tapestries have more than three hundred weft strands to the inch—compared with a count of about one hundred which was the best that was attempted in medieval Europe. (Machine-made worsteds have an equivalent count of seventy to ninety.) Threads were used in natural colors or dyed with vegetable extracts, which produced hues ranging from indigo and red to yellowish brown. Exquisite tapestries with finely toned combinations of colors represent the pinnacle of the early Peruvians' art.

The first Spaniards to see these fabrics were astonished at their quality. Initially it was thought that they were silk, and then it was suggested that the glossy hairs of bats had been used to improve the texture. The truth lay in the patience and skill of the weavers, many of whom spent their entire working lives at the loom. The manufacture of fine tapestries ceased soon after the Conquest, but many of the weavers' skills are still practiced in the highlands of the Andes.

59

6. In Art and Legend

In Inca times there were many different kinds of llamas and alpacas. They were raised for the color of their wool, for their suitability for different regions, and for the part that they were to play on ceremonial occasions. In charge of the flocks in each district was a headman, called the *llama-kamayox*, who supervised the activities of numerous under-herders.

Alpacas were favored for their pure color—dark brown, black, or white. The length and fineness of their wool were also important, with the best animals having coats growing evenly all over the body. The *suri* was developed as a breed for its very long wool, which grows at the rate of about twelve inches a year—it is still an important animal in the highlands of Peru. Among the llamas, the *hueque* or *chilihueque* was a tough race used for carrying water and other heavy burdens in northern Chile.

Llamas of different kinds had an important part to play in the religious and ceremonial life of the Incas. Animals were selected because they represented pure examples of the kinds that could be raised and as such were thought to be the most acceptable to the gods. These animals were sacrificed, often in large numbers, at certain fixed times of the year.

In tracing Inca ceremonies and legends it must be remembered that we soon run into an unknown past. The early Peruvians had no written language, and their history came down through the spoken word; it was only when recounted to the

60

Spaniards that a more permanent record was made. Unfortunately, these accounts are far from complete. Sometimes the Spanish historian was not particularly interested in things about which we would like to know more today, and sometimes events were interpreted in the light of religious ideas of the day. It is also difficult to learn much from the present highland Indian, who is seldom anxious to talk about his beliefs to strangers—even if he has a clear idea in his mind as to why a particular custom is observed.

According to Inca legend, mankind first appeared at Tiahuanaco, near Lake Titicaca. There, on a high rolling plateau of the central Andes, was the cradle of their civilization. There, too, it was believed, were created all the animals, male and female, each molded out of clay. Every year the Incas honored their Creator, Viracocha, at a ceremony in which they sacrificed many llamas. The Sun, or Inti—a supreme deity of the early Peruvians—was also honored, with sacrifices in the richly ornamented temple of Coricancha in Cuzco.

Early in the Inca year (which began about May), a sacred white llama, called the Napa, was escorted into the great plaza of Cuzco. This was part of a magnificent royal ceremony at which the Napa symbolized the first llama to appear on Earth. It was paraded with its own attendants, dressed in a red robe, and with golden ornaments in its ears. This beast enjoyed an honored position throughout its life, and when it died a successor was carefully selected as the new Napa.

Around August, when the fields had been tilled and new crops sown, a further great ceremony was held, this time to drive diseases and evil from the land. Many animals were again brought in for sacrifice, all of which had to be without blemish and with unshorn fleeces. During several days of dancing and feasting the animals were killed and their blood sprinkled over pieces of maize bread carried on golden platters. This bread was

Many hundreds of llamas, specially selected from state-owned flocks, were sacrificed during the course of the Inca year.

eaten by people who had come to Cuzco from the provinces to pay homage to the royal Incas and their deities. It was considered unlucky for anyone not to partake of this sacred food. As the animals were sacrificed their lungs were removed and inflated by the priests, and from their pattern of veins and other signs future events were foretold.

Llamas were regularly used during ceremonial occasions by the Incas for divining or influencing events of the future. The unfortunate animals were sacrificed in attempts to diagnose disease, to forecast the outcome of a war, to test the truth of a confession, and to settle doubtful questions generally. If the onset of the rainy season was delayed, llamas were tied up in open places until they suffered from thirst in the hope that this would appeal to the sympathies of the Thunder God. Sometimes as many as a hundred animals were assembled in Cuzco, awaiting their part in some ceremony, the majority, if not all, of these coming from special flocks maintained by the state.

Underlying these ceremonies there is, to our minds, a pattern of very great cruelty. Probably thousands of llamas and alpacas were killed for ceremonial reasons during the course of the Inca year. They were sacrificed at regular times of the day and on appointed days in the seasonal calendar. Often the color and markings of animals had to be appropriate to the god to whom they were being offered: brown ones to Viracocha, white ones to the Sun, and others with mottled coats to the Thunder or Weather God. Priests led the victims round the image of the deity before the sacrifice was made. Black or dark brown animals were held in high esteem because their muzzles (unlike white animals') matched the color of their coats, and as such they were thought to be more acceptable to the gods.

Every morning, at Cuzco in ancient Peru, a white llama such as this was offered in sacrifice to the sun.

A very different group of people, the Calchaquíes Indians, revered the white guanaco. These were unusual animals and must have been either very pale-fleeced or albinos. Huachi, the Indians said, was a hunter who killed more *talcas* (guanacos) than was necessary. As a punishment the gods took away his son, Rakuy, and banished him to live among the animals. Eventually Rakuy became the Chief of the *Talcas* and, at propitious times, the Calchaquíes believed, he would appear among the mountains as a pure white guanaco.

It was widely believed that the foot of a guanaco and, more especially, the "bezoar stone"—a hard, stony ball of resin and mineral salts that collects in the stomach of lamoids—had magical properties. The bezoar was sucked, or chewed, or taken with an infusion of herbs, and was thought to be effective against poisons and evil spells. The Onas crushed a guanaco bezoar in a mussel shell, and the powder they made was mixed with water, heated, and taken for coughs and lung ailments. The Emperor Charles V of Spain is reputed to have been given bezoar medicine during an illness. In some parts of the Andes, these stones are still carried by the Indians as talismans. Similarly, twists of wool taken from the llama of an enemy are believed to be endowed with magic which can be used in revenge. Clay images of alpacas and llamas are secretly buried in pastures to protect flocks.

Tracing present-day customs associated with the lamoids brings one into touch with some very strange beliefs. What is impressive, I think, is the hold that these ideas still have on the imagination of people. While walking one day through a market in Bolivia I noticed some shriveled bodies of unborn llamas being offered for sale. Such a symbol of unfulfilled life has for the mountain Indians strong magical properties. One buried with the foundations of a house, for instance, brings good fortune to its future inhabitants. Elsewhere, a llama may be sac-

Clay images of alpacas and llamas can be bought in highland markets of Bolivia and Peru. These are believed by the Indians to be endowed with magic and are used to protect their flocks.

rificed when a new house is dedicated. As in former days, the animal is killed facing eastward as the sun rises and its blood smeared on the walls and frames of the building. I have reason to believe that this custom is still practiced in remote parts of Bolivia and Peru, but it is as difficult to find out about this as it is to know what people's thoughts are on such things. There are many stories, for mythology remains unchanged only when people cease to believe in it. Maybe, as a recent traveler has suggested, it is simply as necessary for the highland Indian to bury an embryo of a llama beneath his house as it is to lay the foundations well.

Rather more easy to follow is the llama's part as a pictorial symbol. Throughout the ages it has been a friend of Andean people, and as such it has had a prominent place in the minds of

The stylized form of the suri alpaca, above, its fleece trailing to the ground, appears frequently in ancient Peruvian art.

Golden figurine, left, of a llama dating from Inca times

Peruvian artists. Lamoids have been sculptured in wood and stone; they have been used as a motif to decorate ceramics; and they have been embroidered in textiles. Golden animals graced the gardens of the temples and royal mansions of the Incas, alongside shrubs and flowers all beautifully fashioned in the same precious metal. Figurines and woolen toys representing llamas have been found buried with the dead—possibly as a symbolic source of food in afterlife. Wherever one travels in Peru, one sees the llama as a motif—tall and graceful, very often standing beside a poncho-clad herdsman. The Peruvian flag and coat-of-arms depict the vicuña, and the country's coins, stamps, and seals have all honored the lamoids. In Lima's beautiful Paseo de la República stands a bronze statue of a llama, which to my mind speaks of the high regard for this animal and links the country of today with a rich past.

The statue of Sir Titus Salt at Saltaire commemorates the English manufacturer's achievement in developing machinery for spinning and weaving alpaca wool. An alpaca appears at the base of the column.

7. A New Industry

In the early part of 1836 an English worsted manufacturer named Titus Salt noticed some bales of alpaca wool lying in a Liverpool warehouse. They were rather dirty and uneven in color, having lain there some time—shipped from Peru on the slender chance that a purchaser might be found. There was little interst in alpaca wool at the time, even though it was not new to Britain. Twenty-five years before, William Walton had noted the length and glossy texture of llamas' wool, and in 1830 some yarn had actually been woven at Greetland, near Halifax, and the fabric later sold as a curiosity. But as a commodity the wool had little value. There were technical difficulties in combing and preparing the fibers for spinning, and it was generally felt that they were unsuitable for use in the textile industry.

Titus Salt, who had been born into a textile family and knew some of the problems involved, wondered if machinery could be adapted to handle the new fiber. Before he returned to his home in the Aire Valley in Yorkshire, he acquired a sample to make some experiments. Cleaning and combing this by hand, he spun the fibers into yarn and was astonished at its luster and strength. The wool, he thought, would be suitable for the manufacture of outer garments, and he took some along to show to his father and to a neighboring mill owner. Both advised him to leave it alone, his father in particular begging him to have nothing to do with such "nasty looking stuff."

But Titus Salt clung to his belief in the value of the wool, and he journeyed again to Liverpool to purchase the rest of the consignment of about three hundred bales still lying in the warehouse of Messrs. Hegan, Hall and Company. The purchase caused considerable surprise, and the story was told by Charles Dickens in his magazine *Household Words*. The price paid was eightpence a pound, and after the sale the warehouse owners closed their business for the day in order to give their staff a holiday!

There were many anxious weeks ahead. Alpaca wool has to be thoroughly scoured, or cleaned, before spinning. Furthermore, the glossy nature of the fibers makes them rather slippery, so that the manufacture of yarn by machinery is a delicate and complicated process. But once the problems had been overcome, Titus Salt found that it yielded an even thread with a luster brighter than wool. Its strength and elasticity further confirmed his belief in its suitability for the commercial manufacture of textiles.

Success followed quickly, and before many years alpaca cloth was on drapers' counters throughout the world. Woven with sheep's wool, silk, and cotton, it was made into a range of hard-wearing fabrics. A model manufacturing town called Saltaire grew up round the new Alpaca Works, where more than three thousand people were soon to be employed. Meanwhile, the import of wool from Peru rose to two million pounds annually.

Production continued on a large scale until the end of the nineteenth century when mohair, from Angora goats, softer and more uniform in color, assumed greater importance. Thereafter, alpaca wool was used mainly for outer garments and linings for suits. During the Second World War the demand for alpaca grew again, this time to make the innerlinings of flying clothes for Allied airmen. After the war, synthetic fibers began to be used more and more, and alpaca suffered a new decline—only to be reinstated in recent years by changing fashions. The use of alpaca wool is now on the increase again with the growth of trade in luxury coating fabrics. It has, today, a new variety of uses, blended with the wool of llamas or llama-alpaca hybrids, mixed with sheep's wool for worsteds, or with mohair to produce fancy yarns—all with a characteristic softness and fine sheen.

The main marketing center for the raw wool is Arequipa, in the south of Peru. There, beneath the slopes of the volcano of El Misti, bales of wool are sorted and graded by Indian women and sent to the coast for shipment to North America and

Part of the process of carding, or aligning fibers, prior to spinning alpaca wool

*Weaving alpaca wool at a
modern manufacturing mill
in England*

Europe. The trade brings important revenue to Peru and to the
neighboring land-locked country of Bolivia.

Despite a number of attempts, alpacas have never been suc-
cessfully acclimatized in other countries. They thrive best in the
cool highlands of the Andes, suffering quickly from heat and
disease at lower elevations. On the other hand, the shorter-
haired llama has become familiar in places far away from its
native mountains.

Llamas were used as pack animals in the region of present-day Ecuador during the northern expansion of the Incas in the fifteenth century. There they doubtless helped to carry the blocks of hardened volcanic ash with which much of the early city of Quito was built. Further north in Ecuador, the countryside becomes more humid with the characteristic uplands being known as *páramos*. These damp, mist-swept Andean plateaus are generally unsuitable for llamas, although it is interesting to find that a place near Pasto in Colombia is called Páramo de Guanaco—suggesting that the wild lamoid once reached that point about a hundred miles to the north of the equator. It is possible that llamas lived farther to the north than has been widely supposed; in any event, the arrival of horses, better adapted to the lush highlands of the equatorial Andes, would have rapidly ended their use in these fringe areas soon after the Spanish Conquest.

There are still some two thousand llamas left in the south of Ecuador, where the land is arid like that of northern Peru. The animals are mostly on private estates which have owned herds

Llamas recently introduced into the National Park of Cotopaxi in Ecuador are corralled at night as a protection against dogs and other predators. Although generally silent, llamas call with a kind of bleat—a very different sound from the shrill neigh of wild lamoids.

for many years. Very few, if any, are now used in the country for carrying burdens. A herd of about fifty animals is established on the slopes of the volcano of Cotopaxi, a national park near the Ecuadorian capital of Quito.

Llamas have been taken to other temperate regions of the world, notably to the United States, Great Britain, Ireland, South Africa, and Australia, but with indifferent success. Their introduction to New South Wales in Australia over a century ago was undertaken in the hope of creating a new woolen industry. It is a rather curious tale.

About the time that the Saltaire Alpaca Works was nearing completion in England, Charles Ledger approached the governor of New South Wales with a proposal to import llamas and alpacas from Peru. Ledger was an enterprising man and he had no difficulty in securing the support he needed. Later, he claimed that the governor, Sir Charles FitzRoy, had promised him a grant of ten thousand acres if he brought a hundred alpacas into the colony. Around the middle of the 1850s he set off on his mission to South America.

The first problem he encountered was a ban imposed by the government of Peru on the export of alpacas and llamas. To overcome this, Ledger decided very simply to smuggle the animals out of the country. Assembling a herd at an estate high in the mountains near the Bolivian border, he drove the animals southward across Bolivia into Argentina, then over the Andes to the coast of Chile. It was an incredible journey, beset with hardship, which even today would be a major undertaking; the distance is nearly a thousand miles on the map, and it includes some of the most barren country of the Andes. Ledger is reported to have had vicuñas mixed with his herd of llamas and alpacas, and this alone must have created problems on the great trek. Many animals died in a snowstorm crossing the mountains into Chile, and eventually only 336 of an original herd of 600

74

reached the coast near Copiapó; 60 more died on the voyage to Sydney.

Once in Australia, the remainder of the herd settled down and began to breed. Three years later, in 1861, their number had grown to 417, with many of the offspring hybrids between llamas and alpacas. At that point, the undertaking was declared a success with the press enthusiastically announcing that the llama was already acclimatized and that "its wool had become one of the products of Australia." Ledger then sold the herd to the government for £15,000 with the condition that he continue to be responsible for its management. His care of the animals thereafter was good, but apparently he antagonized public service officials to such an extent that he had to be dismissed. Drought and disease then played a hand, causing the death of many animals, and the government decided to disband the herd. The animals were offered for sale but, as this brought little response, many were eventually given away to farmers. For some years afterwards llamas could be seen in small groups grazing the kangaroo-haunted scrublands of Queensland and New South Wales. Finally, the last remnants were gathered together and taken into zoological gardens. Ledger, for all his unorthodox ways, was widely acclaimed for his enterprise in bringing the animals to Australia, and he received medals from learned societies and from the International Exhibition of London in 1862.

The introduction of lamoids to the Falkland Islands presented fewer problems, since the vegetation and climate were similar to those of the Patagonian mainland three hundred miles away. The raising of guanacos on these cool Atlantic islands seemed a worthwhile idea as early as the 1840s when the governor, Richard Moody, suggested that the experiment should be attempted by some enterprising settler. Subsequently animals were taken over, and they survived for many years. In the early

Staats Island (foreground) in the Falklands where guanacos have been established since they were introduced in the 1930s. A favorite food of the animals on the island is mountain crowberry.

1930s, a further group was put on Staats Island in West Falkland, and there they may be seen today, breeding and evidently thriving.

When one considers how frequently lamoids are seen in zoological collections, it is perhaps surprising that they have not been more widely introduced overseas. The reason is largely that sheep are more satisfactory and popular with farmers from the point of view of commercial wool production. The trying ways of llamas and alpacas suggest that they have not gone so far along the road to domestication. It requires the legendary patience of the highland Indian to do very much with them, and even then the life of whole families may be devoted to looking after and tending the animals.

76

8. Livestock of the Indians

My first acquaintance with llamas in their native land was in the high desert country of western Bolivia. I had traveled there by train, arriving toward dusk one evening at the little frontier town of Charaña. It was a cold and bleak place, where people sat huddled in doorways, and lanterns flickered in dim buildings. But next morning, in the light of the early sun, it seemed a very different world: smoke curled gently into a blue sky, and llamas grazed in a landscape of silver-sheened cacti and mountains glazed with snow.

A team of pack llamas presently wended its way into town. The animals were a wonderful assortment of blacks, browns, grays, and whites. Some were spotted and some were blotched, and no two were the same. Several had roguish fringes of wool falling over their eyes, while others, wide-eyed, heads held high, padded along in a disdainful way, giving me detached glances of interest as they passed. Fastened to their backs with woolen cords were bundles of *tola* scrub—used in that high treeless country for fuel. Following the animals came their drivers, the *llameros*, brightly attired in homespun woolens.

In remote parts of the Bolivian and Peruvian highlands, llamas still play their traditional role as friend and servant of the Indian. Their trails crisscross the land, skirting yellow fields edged with the spiky leaves of maguey, winding through valleys which still bear traces of the old terraced fields of the Incas.

The llama is the only native beast of burden domesticated by people of the New World. Like other lamoids, llamas do not forage at night. They feed on the march, or early in the morning before leaving on a journey. If necessary, they will travel two or three days without food. Loads are tied with woolen cords.

Life in these places has changed little throughout the years.

For many Indians, an occasional visit to market is the main contact with the outside world. During the rest of the time a man lives with his family in a quiet valley remote from any but a few neighbors. Among themselves they speak Quechua or Aymara, rather than Spanish. Men wear the traditional poncho, tunic, and knee breeches, often darned and weathered by age but in which one can still see the signs of fine weaving. Women wear shawls, blouses, and bundles of long skirts, brightly hued with the chemical dyes now usually obtainable in markets. The typical headwear of men is a woolen skullcap with earflaps, woven in intricate patterns and decorated with buttons and tassels. Women have a variety of hats from pastel-shaded homburgs and bowlers to plate-shaped monteras adorned with fringes of colored wool.

The homes of these people, like their clothes, vary from region to region. Those belonging to llama- and alpaca-herders are usually simple mud- or stone-walled structures, thatched with coarse grasses. Sometimes a roof has to be weighted down with boulders as a protection against strong winds. One finds these dwellings tucked away in a sheltered valley or fold of the hills, often several together, lying alongside pens for the animals. Inside each house is a single room in which the family cooks, eats, and sleeps. Sometimes guinea pigs, which are raised for food, scamper over the floor. There is little attention to furniture, for the Indians spend much of their days outdoors and are seldom interested in adding to their basic comfort.

At altitudes above 13,000 feet it is too cold for most crops, except perhaps for potatoes and a kind of grain called *quinoa*, and even these have to be grown in protected places. And so, in the highest inhabited parts, Indians depend for their livelihood on herds of alpacas and llamas.

An alpaca herder of the high border country between Chile and Bolivia. Telltale wrinkles etched into his face tell of the hardships of life in this icy land beneath a tropical sun.

The animals are communally owned by a family, although the land itself often belongs to the village and is shared out in accordance with individual family needs. During the day the black, brown, and variegated animals dot hillsides. Watching over them perhaps will be a child or a solitary Indian woman, the latter wrapped in shawls and peacefully spinning wool on a spindle. In the late afternoon, as shadows lengthen over the close-cropped hills, the animals are guided down to their over-night pens.

These are rectangular areas of stamped ground fenced with rock or adobe walls, which protect the animals from dogs, foxes, and marauding pumas. Sometimes an enclosure lies so close to a house that one has the curious sight of llamas striding through the front door on the way to their quarters. There are separate areas for pack animals, females, and any such as the young or sick needing special attention. Once they are in their pens, alpacas and llamas settle down with a little last-minute grumbling and squabbling; next morning, they rise with the sun, ready to be taken back to their pastures.

Crosses between llamas and alpacas are common and, indeed, much of the wool now exported from Peru comes from these hybrids. In the first generation the fleece is heavier than the alpaca's and the wool finer than the llama's, but there is more grease; in succeeding generations the fine quality of the wool disappears. The names of these hybrids are *huarizo* (for the offspring of a female alpaca and a male llama) and *misti* (when the mother is a llama and the father an alpaca). Crossing also occurs between domestic and wild lamoids, although rarely under natural conditions. Their young have double names: llamo-vicuña, llamo-guanaco, paco-vicuña, and paco-guanaco. Of these, the paco-vicuña is the best known.

The true alpaca comes from the south of Peru, adjacent parts of Bolivia, and one or two places in the Andes of Argentina and

Spinning and weaving are the main handicrafts of highland Indians. An Aymará Indian woman weaves a poncho, universal outer garment of the Andes, on a loom stretched between stakes.

northern Chile. It is the most restricted in range of the lamoids. Smaller than the llama, its body is more rounded, the ears are shorter, and the tail is well hidden in the wool. With their long protective coats, alpacas inhabit high swampy terrain that is generally unsuitable for llamas. In dry places, however, alpacas are small in size and their wool loses its fine quality. Two races, the common and *suri,* are distinguished by the length and silki-

81

Long wool gives the alpaca a poodlelike appearance and enables the animal to thrive on rich pastures, watered by frequent snows, in the highlands of Bolivia and Peru.

ness of the wool—"suri" being a name derived from the Quechua for rhea, so-called because the wool is light and soft like the plumage of those birds. Because they live in high and remote places where they seldom see anyone but their herders, alpacas tend to be rather shy.

The herder's year is divided into a rainy season, from about November to March, and a dry period for the rest of the year. Lambing takes place in the rainy season, which corresponds to the central Andean summer. Llamas and alpacas give birth to one, rarely two, young at a time.

Clipping also takes place during the wet season. Daytime temperatures are then at their highest, so that the thick winter coats can be removed with little chance of the animals taking chill. The new wool, moreover, grows quickly at this time of the year. In places where the Indians follow traditional ways, an animal is first tied by its feet for clipping. Elsewhere, three people may be involved, one grasping the animal by its ears while the others strip the wool on each side with flat rectangular knives. Today, in many parts, shears and machinery are used for this work. An alpaca starts to shed its hair naturally in its third year. This is when shearing begins and when the animal produces its best wool. Thereafter, clipping is undertaken every second year until the animal is about ten or eleven years old; thus each alpaca is clipped four or fives times in its life. Each clipping generally yields about six pounds of wool, but the yield from the suri can be as much as ten pounds.

After clipping, the wool is graded and separated into colors.

Held by an ear, an alpaca is stripped of its fleece near Arequipa in the highlands of southern Peru.

Black wool has a ready market as it needs no dyeing. White animals are valued more for their skins, which are sold as rugs in towns frequented by visitors; many of the so-called "llama skins" that one sees offered for sale come in fact from alpacas. The pelts of young animals that die have a use in making toys and fine woolen articles.

With its ancient background, llama and alpaca husbandry is richly molded by tradition. The pattern of daily and seasonal activities is guided by age-long practice handed down from one generation to another. Ways of treating sick animals, for instance, have obscure beginnings, doubtless going back to the days of the Incas. Many Indians believe that diseases have supernatural causes, and that they must therefore be treated by magical means. An ailing llama is given an infusion of herbs according to some ancient recipe. Ingredients for such cures are bought at special stalls in the markets. The burnt and powdered shells of crabs and crayfish are thought to be beneficial in treating certain ailments, and there are many other "medicines" that are little known to outsiders.

The main use of the llama as a pack animal is for carrying tin ore, grain, wool, and other produce across steep and difficult trails. The traditional pack trains with their teams of Indian drivers still ply in some remote regions. One such route lies across the high Bolivian plateau, or Altiplano, where, during an annual trek, blocks of rock salt are transported to valleys in northern Argentina for trading with sugar, sweet corn, and other produce of warmer regions.

The useful years of a llama's life are from about three until it is ten or twelve years old. In zoos, animals live until they are twenty or even thirty years of age, but in the Andes they are generally killed for meat when they are too old for useful work. The hides are cured for making bed and floor coverings, sandals, and other leather articles. Animals not used as beasts of burden

Female llamas are generally not used for carrying loads and are shorn regularly, although the coarse wool has no great value.

are generally shorn, although the hair has a coarse texture. Occasionally, one sees pack animals being plucked on the march, a handful at a time, and the wool spun on hand spindles by accompanying women. In the Altiplano dung is collected and used as fuel, being known as *takia,* or, in Spanish, *carbón peruano* (Peruvian coal), which burns with little smoke or odor. Llama dung has also been used since early times as a fertilizer. Long dependence on their animals has taught the highland Indians to waste little.

Traditionally, male llamas are employed for carrying burdens. The wool of the back is allowed to grow long and thick so as to form a kind of natural saddle blanket. Depending on its size, a llama carries from 75 to 130 pounds, evenly distributed on both

Guanacos make trusting pets when they are young, playing endlessly and tirelessly with Indian children.

sides of its back. On the march they seldom cover more than twenty miles a day, often much less, picking their way in clustered groups behind a lead llama, which often wears a collar with a bell. It is a fine sight with the colorful *llameros* sprinkled among the animals. Frequent stops are made to allow the animals to graze, for llamas normally eat only during the day. Marching with a llama caravan tends to be leisurely and unhurried.

The *llamero* is always gentle with his animals, encouraging them along with soft words, low whistles, and by waving a cord of colored wool. A faltering beast is helped, and if necessary a halt is called to allow it to rest. The relationship is a pleasant one to see—and one that is in contrast to the noisy ways of many muleteers in the Andes.

Llamas respond to gentleness, but they remain awkward and temperamental, never showing the affection that a horse will toward its owner. The llama cannot be used as a draft animal; neither is it suitable for riding (it is very much smaller than the camel with a weight of about 330 pounds, as compared with 2,200 pounds). A llama with a person on its back quickly tires, sometimes emphasizing its feelings by turning round and spitting into the rider's face.

Highland children grow up with llama lambs, caressing and playing with them as pets. Affection is instilled at an early age, and the children learn to look upon llamas as a symbol of their family's well-being. A certain love of tradition is bestowed on the animals, expressed in gay trappings and colored tassels hanging from their ears. These serve as the owner's markers as well as adornment, but to the visitor they give a certain toyland feeling to that ancient and austere land.

9. The Golden-fleeced Vicuña

Saving the vicuña from extinction has been one of the major success stories of conservationists in recent years. As late as the 1960s its numbers were so low that there were gloomy fears that it would follow the way of the dodo and its woolly-haired ancestors of the North American plains. From the million or more that roamed the Andes in Inca times only scattered groups remained, and these totaled no more than a few thousand individuals. Still they were being hunted and killed for their wool, which fetched ever higher prices on the world market.

Under the Incas the vicuña was revered as the daughter of Pachamama, the goddess of fertility. It had complete protection, with no one allowed to touch an animal except in one of the orderly state-run hunts; to do so carried the penalty of death for having broken the Incas' law. All this changed with the Spanish conquest of Peru after 1532. Old laws were swept aside and nothing took their place. There was much wanton killing, with reports of eighty thousand animals being slaughtered a year. As early as 1602 one of Peru's leading writers, the "Inca" Garcilaso, wrote that there were hardly any vicuñas (or guanacos) left except in areas where it was difficult to use guns. To make matters worse there was growing competition for forage and space from domestic sheep and alpacas. Harassment by dogs was now a threat, especially to the mother vicuñas and their young. During the seventeenth and eighteenth centuries

A royal animal in ancient Peru, the vicuña has a prominent place in that country's coat-of-arms.

the decline continued and then, in 1825, Simón Bolívar, the hero of South American independence, issued a law (the first of its kind for nearly three hundred years) protecting the vicuña. This forbade the slaughter in Peru, a country soon to adopt the animal on its national emblem. Unfortunately, these good intentions largely went unheeded, particularly in remote places where the law could not be enforced.

With supplies of the precious wool diminishing, interest turned to raising the animals in captivity. This promised to be very profitable, but difficulties were soon encountered. Deeply ingrained in the vicuña's nature is the aggressive instinct which adapts it to life on the barren puna, each little group spaced well away from its neighbors. Herded together in fenced pastures, vicuñas become unnaturally vicious, biting, kicking, and fighting among themselves. Under these conditions they do not breed. A possible solution, it was thought, might be found in trying to raise hybrids between vicuñas and the more docile alpacas.

An early attempt to establish the paco-vicuña as a breed was made by a priest, Father Cabrera. About 1845, after more than twenty years of patient work, he managed to rear a small herd of these animals in the mountains near Macusani in southern Peru. This seemed promising, for the wool was almost as fine as the vicuña's and there was much more of it. Unfortunately, these animals did not breed true. In other words, their offspring, in the second or third generations, became more like vicuñas or alpacas, and their value was lost. The experiment was not a success, but Father Cabrera was commended for his work by the government of Peru.

Interest in raising paco-vicuñas continued, although the growth of knowledge about genetics and inheritance was beginning to shed some light on the nature of the problems involved. The most famous name linked with new attempts to establish vicuña crosses and to domesticate the vicuña was Juan Francisco Paredes.

Don Juan Paredes was a landowner from the Puno district near Lake Titicaca. In 1919, he released ten young vicuñas into an enclosed area on his estate. This group was added to from time to time as further young animals were caught, but it was only after eighteen years that the first ranch-bred vicuña was born. However, this was quickly followed by others, and when the estate became a research center of the Peruvian government in 1969 several hundreds had already been raised. The experiment, although noteworthy, is considered by wildlife specialists as only a partial success. The animals live in what might be described as semiconfined protection and still retain their strong territorial instincts. A new problem is the fact that a skin disease called mange is more easily transmitted from one animal to another. This means that they have to be rounded up once a year when, in a modern version of the *chaco*, Indian herdsmen drive the animals into a corral to be checked, treated, and later released.

Paredes managed to cross female alpacas with male vicuñas by raising intended pairs together from infancy. More than two hundred of these paco-vicuña hybrids were born. At first the results seemed encouraging but, like Father Cabrera, he found that succeeding generations did not hold the characteristics of the original crosses. Moreover, many animals did not breed at all. Further attempts have since been made, but a satisfactory breeding stock has yet to be achieved.

Most of us would agree that the first need is to try to preserve vicuñas in the wild. A series of field studies by scientists during the years 1957-1971 yielded important information about the size and habits of surviving populations, and from this plans were developed for the vicuña's future. Much of the work was coordinated by the International Union for Conservation of Nature, with the financial help of such organizations as the World Wildlife Fund and the Frankfurt Zoological Society. In 1971, an international conference on vicuña conservation was held in Peru to review these activities.

For a long time the situation had been very confused. Officially, vicuñas were protected in Peru and Bolivia, but the skins were still sold openly in both countries. Vicuña rugs and blankets, for instance, appeared regularly in souvenir shops, and industrialized countries imported the wool, overlooking the fact that it had been smuggled out of its country of origin. The first real progress was made when Felipe Benavides, a Peruvian naturalist, began a nationwide campaign to try to save the vicuña. He sought the help of overseas governments to ban imports of vicuña products, and he impressed upon authorities nearer home the need to set up reserves.

Felipe Benavides, a noted Peruvian naturalist, who has done much to ensure better protection for the vicuña

The first vicuña reserve to come into existence was Pampa Galeras, an area of rolling, treeless grassland in the mountains to the southeast of Lima. This was set aside in 1963. A notable feature about its creation was that much of the land was set aside by the people of the nearby Indian village of Lucanas, who agreed not to allow domestic animals to graze there. The scheme quickly became a success, with the number of vicuñas growing from one thousand to twenty-two thousand (in 1976)— a splendid tribute to the far-sighted action of conservationists and these highland people.

Perhaps the greatest obstacle that remains is the continuing trade in skins and vicuña products. These are smuggled out of the country in a variety of ways, sometimes hidden in bales of sheep's wool. Stories of these graceful creatures being slaughtered with automatic guns bring home to us the awful aspects of the problem. The governments of Peru and her neighboring countries are taking strong action to control this, with long terms of imprisonment for offenses. Bolivia, for instance, has strengthened laws and set up a reserve in the pampa of Ulla Ulla, near the border with Peru, which has helped to control an important route used by the smugglers. The United States and Great Britain have banned the import of vicuña wool, and it is hoped that other countries will take similar steps. But to keep the trade in check requires constant vigilance on the part of governments, air companies, and shipping lines. The most hopeful prospect lies in the Convention on International Trade in Endangered Species, which aims at preventing trade in many rare plants and animals throughout the world.

I mentioned earlier that the progress so far has been en-

An agreement, signed in La Paz in 1970 between representatives of Argentina, Bolivia, Chile, and Peru, gave complete protection to the vicuña. At Pampa Galeras in Peru numbers have been increasing by some 25 to 30 percent each year. In 1976 there were an estimated 22,000 in the reserve.

Although responding well to protection by man, vicuñas usually refuse to breed in captivity. Their future lies in adequate reserves and the careful management of wild populations, such as was practiced in the days of the Incas.

couraging. Besides the pampas at Galeras and Ulla Ulla, there are now vicuña reserves at Lauca in northern Chile and in the mountains of San Juan province in Argentina. In all the countries where the vicuña lives, it is now fully protected and there are special areas set aside for it. Peru has a second reserve, called Aguada Blanca, on the high puna near El Misti in the province of Arequipa. By 1976, the number of vicuña in the country had grown to about thirty thousand. Encouraged by this success, the Ecuadorian authorities are hoping to re-establish vicuñas in their country, on the spectacular volcanic slopes of the Cotopaxi National Park.

The prospects for this little lamoid with the golden fleece are brighter now than they have been for many years. But one wonders what the distant future holds, for the pressures of land

94

use and colonization are certain to spread. Like many other freedom-loving creatures, it lives in a shrinking world. Ultimately, much depends upon the future and welfare of the people of the Altiplano, for their destinies have long been linked. The best chance lies in careful management of vicuña populations, such as was practiced in the days of the Incas. Wool sheared from the wild animals, and meat and hides obtained by cropping surplus males would provide a livelihood for people who, at present, live in poverty. The vicuña is able to thrive at higher elevations than domestic animals and on land where agriculture is hard and uneconomical. However intolerant it may be of captivity, it seems to respond well to protection by man. In this way the vicuña may yet roam again in places where its ancestors lived long, long ago.

Index